See it –

COPYRIGHT

Published by...Independently published on KDP Amazon.....
© Copyright @ John James 2017
John James has asserted his right under the copyright, designs and patents act, 1988 to be identified as the author of this work.
This book is sold subject to the conditions that it shall not, by way of trade or otherwise, be lent, resold, hired out, or otherwise circulated without the publishers prior consent in any form of binding or cover other than that in which it is published and without a similar condition being imposed on the subsequent purchaser.
First published in. Oct 2017.....
by...Independently published on KDP Amazon

Amazon ISBN 9781549937552

See it – say it Spanish

ACKNOWLEDGEMENTS

Aug 2017

I wrote this book with the express aim of assisting others to learn 'Basic Spanish'
in a simple, easy to understand and fun way....

My grateful thanks to.....

Firstly, My wife Annette, who has put up with me, constantly talking things over with myself and working long hours on the computer, and what would seem very much like obsessing over everything during the writing of this book

secondly to my Spanish teacher's, who have very patiently put up with my incessant questions, over the years. Tamara, who now lives in UK with her husband and child, and Laura, who still teach's and advises me

See it – say it Spanish

OTHER BOOKS BY THE SAME AUTHOR:

'Talk to me - conversational Spanish'

Learn basic conversational Spanish with a twist.....
Everyday conversations broken down and analysed..
So that you not only learn what to say, but, why you say it that way ,and what reactions / comments / questions to expect.

Also - 'Buenos para saber' (bwen-os para sab-air) good to know's,
Tips on the lifestyle, culture and habits of the Spanish peoples

See it – say it Spanish

CONTENTS:

No.	Content	page.
1.	Introduction	05
2.	How to use this book`	08
3.	Spanish alphabet and rules	12
4.	Numbers	13
5.	Present tense; a. Regular ar, er and ir verbs	17
6.	X-search	38

7.	End of lesson drills
	   a. Final practice
	   b. Summary
	   c. Look forward
		42
		42
		49
		50

8.	Index ; most common regular verbs	52
9.	Answers for exercises	55
10.	About the author	69
11.	Intentionally left blank	70

See it – say it Spanish

INTRODUCTION

Welcome to the 1st book in the *'See it - Say it'* Basic Spanish series. The main aim of this series of books is to help you to learn basic Spanish in a simple and easy to understand way....

Why did I write this book in the first place ?
I started learning Spanish at 'night classes' at the local college on one evening a week for 2 hours at a time. I very quickly realised that although the teacher was (and a lot of the books I had bought) presenting me with a multitude of facts , verbs, conjugations and lots of other clutter......'STOP' !!! I didn't need all this other stuff around when I wanted to learn the basics. Also very few of the books had any feedback (practice) method (you will use self testing throughout this series, so that you can use and see at a glance how you are progressing) and feedback (practice) is very IMPORTANT.

What do I hope to achieve with it ?
My hope is to assist anyone in their first steps of learning Spanish in a simple and easy to understand way, and to encourage them to going beyond the basics, and possibly into becoming quite a fluent Spanish speaker.

See it – say it Spanish

How will you benefit from this book ?
I will give you the important basics needed for learning stage by stage, taking away all the clutter that can be found in some books. You will have the opportunity to self test and see for yourself how quickly you progress.

How will you do this ?
You will be using a tried and tested method that I used successfully for many years in the Army...***E.D.I.P, explanation, demonstration, imitation, practice.***
Each book will deal with a different aspect of the basics of Spanish....allowing you to learn and master each part without the clutter of other stuff to distract you.

The pronunciations of words / verbs will be broken down to allow easy understanding. Interspersed throughout the books will be interesting facts about life in Spain, whether you are simply interested, going on holiday or contemplating a more permanent situation, these will appear in text boxes called:

'*buenos para saber*'   (bwen-oss para sab-air)

translated it means   **'Good to knows'**

There are also some fun **'X-search'** boxes that combine the fun of a crossword and the frustration of a word search with clues in English and Spanish.

it is important that you turn over and read **' how to use this book'** as it will explain quite a lot and hopefully avoid any confusion

That's enough waffle from me . Go ahead and start what I believe will be your beginning to an enjoyable journey to learning the Spanish language....

with......

'See it - Say it' Basic Spanish.

See it – say it Spanish

HOW TO USE THIS BOOK

The main aim of this series of books is to help you to learn basic Spanish in a simple, easy to understand way....

Why did I write these books in the first place ?
Well , you see...I consider myself fairly intelligent; however some of the explanations in most books that I read when I first started to learn Spanish, written by very educated academics, and I believe were only meant for academics, left me floundering. I thought.. ....**there has to be an easier way** to learn how to speak basic Spanish. So I embarked upon this task, firstly for a few friends who had not seen the inside of a classroom for many a year, and the prospect frightened the life out of them, I wrote this first book, and it proved to be such a success, I thought maybe I can help others in the same way.

In English we have 2 sounds to every letter..A & a, B & b. The capital letter/uppercase (*mayúsculo - may-yoos-koo-loh*) and the baby sounds for lowercase (*minísculo - meen-ees-koo-loh*) The Spanish don't, they only have the lowercase sounds. This actually makes it easier to learn.

The pronunciation of Spanish words is very important, placing the emphasis on the wrong vowel (a, e, i, o, u) can either make no sense at all, or mean something absolutely different.

See it – say it Spanish

In English it is a simple matter to know who is doing / saying what....we use the prefix **I, he, she, they, it, they all , we all or you all** .

The Spanish don't..they change the end of the verb to let you know who is doing / saying what, whether it be at the present, in the past, or will be in the future, who could, should or would do. This is called a 'conjugation ' (*kon-joo-gay-shun*)

So when a Spanish verb is changed to say who....it is said to be 'conjugated'

eg: **Hablar** (*ab-lah*) to talk   (h is always silent)

when I drop the **'ar'** and add **'o'** to make **hablo** it is conjugated to let you know that **'I talk'**

Throughout these **' See it-say it Spanish'** books, how to pronounce the words in Spanish will appear in (***phonetics'***) within brackets after the word.........it will be broken down and separated by a, - *(*dash*)*, and the vowel to stress or emphasise will be highlighted in ***red*****.....**

Eg: penguin   -   Pingüino (***peen-goo-een-o***)

Firstly say each part separately, and then repeat a few times, putting them closer together until the complete word is achieved

See it – say it Spanish

Throughout the book, how to say the word / verb uses the following......

...-**ah**- makes the same sound as the ar in   **car**
...-**air**- makes the same sound as the air in   h**air**
..-**eer**- makes the same sound as the eer in   **beer**
.-**are**- makes the same sound as the are in   **share**

Your first phrase to learn and **repeat every day**.......
 ' **Puedo   hacerlo** ' (*pw-air-doh   ath-air-lo*)
Translation: **I CAN DO IT !!**

At the end of each phase there will be a small self test, to allow you to see how well you are doing. It's always a good idea to try and attain a certain level before moving on.....I have placed a box at the end of each test, It looks like this one on the right....
Always use a pencil each time that you test yourself
Place your score in the space in the box, the next time you will be able to see at a glance how you have progressed.....

```
          ___
           10
```

All answers can be found at the back of the book, commencing from page 43

When you see, **eg:**   this means that what follows is an example of what has been taught

E.D.I.P.

My method of instruction follows the adage that I learnt and used in the Army, it is a proven method that is simple and easy to use, and that is **E.D.I.P.**

E. **Explanation......**
I will try to explain things as simply as I can stage by stage

D. **Demonstration.....**
Using easy to understand examples, I will demonstrate how what I explained is used
/ put into practice.

I. **Imitation.......**
.At each stage You will imitate what has been taught in the form of self- testing.

P. **Practice..........**
This where you will practice everything from that stage through self-testing

At the end of the book you will have the opportunity to carry out a final practice that will include a mixture of all that you have learned

It is **really important** that you understand fully, each stage, **before** you move on to the next stage

I believe that the real secret to learning is... **Practice.....Practice....Practice....**

And more practice.........!!!!!!!!!

Now **go......** and learn Basic Spanish quickly and easily ....and remember.......

'Puedo hacerlo'

See it – say it Spanish

BASIC SPANISH - ALPHABET

a =	*a*	n =	*en-e*
b =	*be*	ñ =	*en-ye*
c =	*th-e*	o =	*o*
ch=	*ch-e*	p =	*pay*
d =	*de*	q =	*koo*
e =	*e*	r =	*air-e*
f =	*ef-e*	s =	*ess-e*
g =	*ghe*	t =	*tay*
h =	*achay*	u =	*oo*
i =	*ee*	v =	*oo-bay*
j =	*hoe-ta*	w=	*oo-bay-dob-lay*
k =	*kar*	x =	*ek-iss*
l =	*el-e*	y =	*ee-gree-a-gar*
ll =	*el-ye*	z =	*theta*
m =	*em-e*		

RULES:
within words:
c before i or e…..pronounced as 'th' *
    eg: cerveca (beer) **th-air-bay-tha**
g before i or e….pronounced as the ch in 'lo<u>ch</u>'
h is <u>always</u> silent
eg:hotel (**o-tel**), ola – (hola - hello) **o-lar**, ablar – (to speak) **ab-lar**
i **always** pronounced …ee
j before all vowels is pronounced as an 'h' or as the ch in 'loch'
    eg: Jugar – (to play) **hoo-gar**, trabajar-(to work) **trab-a-har**
v is like a b (see c – cerveca - **th-air-<u>bay</u>-tha**)
x is pronounced as x as in 'extra'
z is always pronounced as 'th'

See it – say it Spanish

Note: * - in some parts of spain, c+i or e, or z are pronounced as an **s** eg: (*s-air-bay-sa*) *beer*

BASIC SPANISH – NUMBERS

1 = UNO   (*OO-NO*)
2= DOS   (*D-OS*)
3= TRES   (*TRES*)
4= CUATRO   (*KWOT-ROE*)
5= CINCO   (*THEEN-CO*)
6= SEIS   (*SAY-SS*)
7= SIETE   (*SAY-AY-TAY*)
8= OCHO   (*OT-CHO*)
9= NUEVE   (*NEW-AY-BAY*)
10= DIEZ   (*DEE-ETH*)
11- ONCE   (*ON-THAY*)
12= DOCE   (*DOE-THAY*)
13= TRECE   (*TRE-THAY*)
14= CATORCE   (*CAT-OR-THAY*)
15= QUINCE   (*KIN-THAY*)
16= DIECISEIS   (*DEE-ETH-EE-SAYS*)
17= DIECISIETE(*DEE-ETH-EE-SAY-AY-TAY*)
18= DIECIOCHO   (*DEE-ETH-EE-OCHO*)
19= DIECINUEVE(*DEE-ETH-EE-NEW-AY-BAY*)
20= VEINTE   *BENT-AY*)
21= VEINTIUNO   (*BENT-EE-OOH-NO*)
22= VEINTIDOS   (*BENT-EE-DOS*)
23= VEINTITRES   (*BENT-EE-TRES*)
24= VEINTICUATRO (*BENT-EE-KWAT-RO*)
25= VEINTICINCO (*BENT-EE-THEEN-CO*)

Numbers 21 to 29 are said as in English : 21, 22, 23, etc.

From 31 onwards it is said as:
30 and 1,
30 and 2,
40 and 1,
40 and 2,
70 and 5,
80 and 7
Etc....

See it – say it Spanish

26= VEINTISEIS   (***BENT-EE-SAY-SS***)
27= VEINTISIETE   (***BENT-EE-SAY-AY-TAY***)
28= VEINTIOCHO   (***BENT-EE-OT-CHO***)
29= VEINTINUEVE(***BENT-EE-NEW-AY-BAY***)

30= TREINTA   (***TREE-ENTA***)
40= CUARENTA   (***KWAR-ENTA***)
50= CINCUENTA   (***THEEN-KWENTA***)
60= SESENTA   (***SES-ENTA***)
70= SETENTA   (***SET-ENTA***)
80= OCHENTA   (***OTCH-ENTA***)
90= NOVENTA   (***NO-BENTA***)
100= CIEN   (***THEE-EN***)
100+= CIENTO.   (***THEE-ENTO***)
200= DOSCIENTOS (***DOS-THEE-ENTOS***)
300= TRESCIENTOS (***TRES-THEE-ENTOS***)
400= CUATROCIENTOS(***KWAT-RO-THEE- ENTOS***)
500= QUINIENTOS   (***KIN-EE-ENTOS***)
600= SEISCIENTOS (***SAY-SS-THEE-ENTOS***)
700= SIETECIENTOS (***SAY-AY-TAE-THEE-ENTOS***)
800= OCHOCIENTOS (***OCHO-THEE-ENTOS***)
900= NOVECIENTOS (***NOBE-THEE-ENTOS***)
1000= MIL   (***MEEL***)
(*1,000/3,00 =una /dos/tres meel etc..*)
1,000,000 MILLÓN   (***MEE-YON)***

See it – say it Spanish

SIMPLE COMMON USAGE WORDS :

Greeting's and farewell's

Hello	= hola	*(oh-lah)*
Goodbye	= adios	*(ad-ee-yos)*
good morning	= buenos dias	*(bwen-os dee-as)*
good afternoon /evening	= buenas tardes	*(bwen-as tahr-des)*
Goodnight (greeting as well)	= buenas noches	*(bwenas notch-es)*
Until tomorrow	= hasta mañana	*(asta man-yar-n)*
Until later / see you later	= hasta luego	*(asta loo-ay-go)*
Until soon / see you soon	= hasta pronto	*(asta pronto)*

Other useful words

Thank you	= gracias	*(grath-ee-as)*
Please	= por favour	*(por-fabor)*
Coffee, white	= café con leche	*(caf-ay con lech-ee)*
Coffee, black	= café solo	*(caf-ay solo)*
Tea	= té	*(tay)*
Water	= agua	*(agwa)*
With	= con	
Without	= sin	
milk	= leche	*(letch-ee)*
Sugar	= azúcar	*(ath-oo-car)*
Beer	= cerveza	*(th-air-bay-tha)*
Ice	= hielo	*(ee-yelo)*
And	= y	*(ee)*

See it – say it Spanish

Note: * if you want tea with milk, ask for...
'té con poco leche fria' *(tay con poco de lech-ee free-a)*

Some useful phrases

Where are the toilet s ? = dondestan al aseos
                          (donde-estan al ass-ay-os)

What time is it ?   = que hora es **(kay orra es)**

At what time ?   = a que hora **(a kay orra)**

Where is the town hall? = donde es la ayuntamiento
                          (.ayun- ta-mee-ento)
What time does the shop open / close...?
         = a que hora la tienda esta abierta / cerrad
(a-kay orra la-tee-enda esta ab-ee-air- ta / th-air-ar-da)

How much is it   = cuanto cuesta / cuanto vale
                    (kwonto kwesta   or kwonto baa-lee)
In the morning   = por la mañana   **(por la man-yarna)**
In the afternoon = por la tarde   **(por la tarr-day)**
At night   = por la noche   **(por la notch-ay)**

today	= Hoy	(*oi*)
yesterday	= Ayer	*(eye-air)*
last night	= Anoche	*(a-notch-ay)*
tomorrow	= Mañana	*(man-yarna)*

See it – say it Spanish

> **Buenos para saber ...**
> (.good to knows - **bwen-oss para sab-air**)
> In Spanish when a question mark ?, or an exclamation mark ! Is used ...there is always an inverted (upside down) mark placed at the beginning of the question or statement / comment as well...
> eg:
> ¿ donde has estado?   (*don-day ass ess-tar-doh*)
>   Where have you been ?
>
> ¡ gracias a dios!   (*grath-ee-ass a dee-oss*)
>   Thank God !

SPANISH VERB'S.

All Spanish verbs (doing words) end in either: **ar, er** or **ir**

<u>**HABLAR**</u> = <u>to speak</u>
<u>**VIVIR**</u>   = <u>to live</u>
<u>**COMER**</u>   = <u>to eat</u>

All verbs can be conjugated (changed) to say who is doing what.

To conjugate the verb we simply drop the *ar, er* or *ir* leaving only the stem

And add the ending relevant to who is doing / saying, For instance:...

See it – say it Spanish

eg:	HABLAR	COMER	VIVIR
I	habl-**o**	com-**o**	viv-**o**
You	habl-**as**	com-**es**	viv-**es**
he/she/it	habl-**a**	com-**e**	viv-**e**
We	habl-**amos**	com-**emos**	viv-**imos**
you all	habl-**ais**	com-**eis**	viv-**is**
They	habl-**an**	com-**en**	viv-**en**

When pronouncing a full verb (un-conjugated) the emphasis is on the last vowel
(**a, e, i, o,** or **u**) spoken.

Hablar / com**e**r / viv**i**r / sal**i**r / beb**e**r

Eg: hablar = *ab-laah* / comer = *kom-air*
    vivir = *bee-beer* / Salir = *sal-eer*
    beber = *beb-air*

Hablar	*to speak*
Comer	*to eat*
Vivir	*to live*
Salir	*to leave*
Beber	*to drink*

remember:
*the **'h'** is always silent*
*i pronounced as **'ee'***
*v, as a soft **'b'***

See it – say it Spanish

When pronouncing the verbs, stating who is doing the action, in English we use *I, you, he, she, it, they, we,* in Spanish the verb is conjugated (changed) with the emphasis placed on the penultimate (*last but one*) vowel

Hablo - hablamos
como - comemos
vivo - vivimos

So first we have to understand the Spanish words **for who or whom** is doing the action.....

I (me)	= yo	(*joe*)
You	= tu	(*too*)
He/she/it	= el /ella	(*el / ay-ah*) *
We	= nosotros	(*no-sot-ross*)
You all	= vosotros	(*bow-sot-ross*)
They	= ellos / ellas	(*ay-yoss / ay-yass*) **

* *el / ellos* are masculine (masculino - ***mass-koo-lee-no***),
   lo is used for he or it. *Ellos* is for more than one male

** *la(s) / ella(s)* are feminine (femenino – ***fem-en-neeno***)
   la is used for she. *Ellas* is for more than one female

See it – say it Spanish

** both **el** and **la**, **ellos** or **ellas** are used for other words depending on the number and gender, whether they are classified as male or female, more about that in a later booklet.

Note: if there are a mixture of males and females the masculine form takes precedence...

eg: **(1)** there are 13 females and 1 male student in the class, they are referred to as ellos. **(2)** if the genders are not known, ellos is used.

we will start with the AR verbs:

AR verbs - present tense (NOW)

All *ar* verbs in the present tense have the same endings: Simply drop the *ar*, which leaves the stem, eg: hablar becomes **habl** - and add one of the following:

Yo	-o	(*oh*)
tu	-as	(*ass*)
el / la	-a	(*a*)
nosotros	-amos	(*arm-os*)
vosotros	-ais	(*ice*)
ellos/ellas	-an	(*ann*)

See it – say it Spanish

these endings can be applied to almost all **ar** verbs

---

so, to conjugate a verb...we remove the 'ar', 'er', 'ir' and add either the...
o, for me, - **as,** for you, - **a,** for he /she/it,
amos, for we, - **ais,** for you all, - **an** for they

eg:	**Habl-ar**		
yo	habl-**o**	I speak	(*aa-blow*)
tu	habl-**as**	you speak	(*aa-blass*)
el/la	habl-**a**	he/she/it speaks	(*aa-bla*)
nosotros	habl-**amos**	we speak	(*ab-lar-mos*)
vosotros	habl-**ais**	you all speak	(*aa-blice*)
ellos/ellas	habl-**an**	they speak	(*aa-blan*)

Remember:
The Spanish language is phonetic (***fon-etic***) it does not have lower and upper case sounds ....only lower case:

See it – say it Spanish

AR VERB DRILLS

we will now practice what we have learned so far.....

fill in the blanks with the conjugated verbs....

eg: mirar...(mee-rah)) .... to watch / look

Yo __MIRO_____ tu __MIRAS_____ el/ella MIRA_____Nosotros __MIRAMOS_ / vosotros _MIRAIS___ los/ellas __MIRAN_____ ,

Now try these:...

1. Cantar...(*can-taah*) .... to sing

Yo _____/ tu _____/el/ella _____ , Nosotros _____ ,

vosotros _____ / ellos/ellas _____ ,

2. Andar (*an-daah*) ..... to walk

Yo _____ / tu _____/ella _____/ nosotros _____

vosotros _____ / ellos/ellas _____

3. Bailar (*bye-laah*) to dance

Yo _____ ,/ tu _____ /el/ella _____/ Nosotros _____

vosotros _____ ,/ ellos/ellas _____

22

See it – say it Spanish

4. Nadar (*na-daah*) to swim

Yo _____ / tu _____ /l/ella _____ ,/nosotros _____

vosotros _____ / ellos/ellas _____ ,

5. Tratar (*trat-aah*) to treat

yo _____ /, tu _____ / el/ella _____ ,/Nosotros _____

vosotros _____ / ellos/ellas _____

6. Pasear (*pass-ay-aah*) to walk – for pleasure

Yo _____ /, tu _____ /, el/ella _____ /,Nosotros _____

vosotros _____ / ellos/ellas _____ ,

7. Robar (*rroe-baah*) to rob

Yo _____ , tu _____ el/ella _____ /Nosotros _____

vosotros _____ / ellos/ellas _____

,If 5 out of 6 of each verb are correct, class that one as correct. If total less than 4, go back, and try again....

7

See it – say it Spanish

Lets try something a little harder....

8. Fill in the blanks with either the **English** or **Spanish** form as required.........

*(eg: nado: **I swim** / anda: **you walk** / we dance: **bailamos**)*

I sing _____ / andas _____ tratan _____

they rob _____ / He treats _____

pasean _____ / we sing _____

I walk _____ / Bailais _____

nada _____ / we dance _____

trato _____ / Andan _____

paseais _____ / she robs _____

we swim _____ / Nadas _____

They walk _____ / robo _____

tratamos _____

　　　　　　　　　　　　　　　　　　　　_____

　　　　　　　　　　　　　　　　　　　　20

8 - 10　　average
11 - 14　　above average
15 - 20　　excellent

See it – say it Spanish

Excellent, well done !!!

Now lets move on to the *er* verbs

As with the **ar** verbs we simply drop the **er** and leave the stem....then add the following endings......

Me	(yo)	-o	(***oh***)
You	(tu)	-es	(***ess***)
He/she/it	(el/la)	-e	(***eh***)
We	(nosotros)	-emos	(***air-moss***)
You all	(vosotros)	-eis	(***ace***)
They	(ellos/ellas)	-en	(***enn***)

these endings can be applied to almost all *er* verbs

remember:

o, for me, - **es,** for you, - **e,** for he/she/it,
emos, for we, - **eis,** for you all, - **en** for they

eg 1:	comer		
yo	Com-**o**	I eat	*koe-moh*
tu	Com-**es**	you eat	*koe-mess*
el/ella	Com-**e**	he/she/it eats	*koe-me*
nosotros	Com-**emos**	we eat	*kom-air-moss*
vosotros	Com-**eis**	you-all eat	*koe-mace*
ellos/ellas	Com-**en**	they eat	*koe-men*

See it – say it Spanish

eg 2: beber

yo	beb-**o**	I drink	**beb-oh**
tu	beb-**es**	you drink	**beb-ess**
el/ella	beb-**e**	he/she/it drinks	**beb-eh**
nosotros	beb-**emos**	we drink	**beb-air-moss**
vosotros	beb-**eis**	you-all drink	**beb-ace**
ellos/ellas	beb-**en**	they drink	**beb-enn**

ER Verb Drills

we will now practice what we have learned so far.....

fill in the blanks with the conjugated verbs....

eg: aprender (a-pren-d-air).... to learn
Yo __APRENDO___   tu APRENDES___ , el/ella __APRENDE__
Nosotros **APRENDEMOS** vosotros **APRENDEIS**_ ellos/ellas **APRENDEN**_

Now try these:..
1.Vender (*ben-d-air*).... to sell

Yo _____/ tu _____ / el/ella _____,/Nosotros _____

vosotros _____ / ellos/ellas _____ ,

2.Leer (*lee-air*) ..... to read

Yo _____/tu _____ e_l/ella _____/,Nosotros _____

vosotros _____/ ellos/ellas _____

See it – say it Spanish

3. Correr (*corr-air*) to run

Yo _____ /tu _____/el/ella _____/,Nosotros _____

vosotros _____ / ellos/ellas _____,

4. Deber (*deb-air*) to owe /must

Yo _____ / tu _____/ el/ella _____/,Nosotros _____

vosotros _____ / ellos/ellas _____

5. Romper (*rom-pair*) to break / tear

Yo _____,/ tu _____/ella _____/,Nosotros _____

vosotros _____ / ellos/ellas ____

6. Responder (*res-pond-air*) to respond / answer

Yo _____/ tu _____/el/ella _____/,Nosotros _____

vosotros _____, / ellos/ellas _____,

7. Temer (*tem-air*) to be afraid / fear

Yo _____/, tu _____/_el/ella _____/,Nosotros _____

vosotros _____ / ellos/ellas _____,

If 5 out of 6 are correct, class that one as correct. If total less than 5, go back, and try again.....

7

See it – say it Spanish

Fill in the blanks with either the *English* or *Spanish* form as required………

(eg: <u>vendeis: you all sell</u> / rompo: I break / they read: leen)

I sell _____ / corres _____ / leen _____

they broke _____ / He breaks _____ / respondeis _____

we run _____ / I read _____ / rompemos _____

debe _____ / we reply _____ / vendemos _____

tememos _____ / corren _____ / he is afraid _____

we owe ____ / lees _____ / They sell _____

responde _____ / leemos _____

```
 8 - 10    average
11 - 14    above average
15 - 20    excellent
```

20

Excellent, well done !!!

Now lets move on to the *ir* verbs

As with the **ar** and **er** verbs we simply drop the **ir** and leave the stem....then add the following endings......

Me	(yo)	-o	(*oh*)
You	(tu)	-es	(*ess*)
He/she/it	(el/ella)	-e	(*eh*)
We	(nosotros)	-imos	(*ee-moss*)
You all	(vosotros)	-is	(*eese*)
They	(ellos/ellas)	-en	(*enn*)

these endings can be applied to almost all *ir* verbs

---

remember:
o, for me, - **es,** for you, - **e,** for he/she/it,
imos, for we, - **is,** for you all, - **en** for they

eg 1:	*partir (to share)*		
yo	part-**o**	I share	*part-oh*
tu	part-**es**	you share	*part-ess*
el/ella	part-**e**	he/she/it share	*part-e*
nosotros	part-**imos**	we share	*part-ee-moss*
vosotros	part-**is**	you-all share	*part-eese*
ellos/ellas	part-**en**	they share	*part-en*

See it – say it Spanish

eg 2:   **insistir** *(to insist)*

yo	insist-**o**	I insist	*enn-seest-oh*
tu	insist -**es**	you insist	*een-seest-es*
el/ella	insist -**e**	he/she/it insist	*een-seest-e*
nosotros	insist -**imos**	we insist	*een-seest-ee-moss*
vosotros	insist -**is**	you-all insist	*een-seest-eese*
ellos/ellas	insist -**en**	they insist	*een-eest-en*

IR Verb Drills
we will now practice what we have learned so far.....

fill in the blanks with the conjugated verbs....

eg: **abrir** *(ab-r-eer)*.... to open
Yo __**ABRO**___ , tu __**ABRES**_____ el/ella __**ABRE**____ ,Nosotros _**ABREMOS**, vosotros _**ABREIS**__ , ellos/ellas __**ABREN**___ ,

Now try these:..

1Reñir (*ren-yeer*).... to quarrel / argue

Yo _____ ./ tu _____ /.el/la _____ ,/Nosotros _____

vosotros _____ , / ellos/ellas _____ ,

2.Escribir (*es-cree-beer*) ..... to write

Yo _____ /tu _____ /_ el/ella _____ /,Nosotros _____

vosotros _____ , / ellos/ellas _____ ,

30

See it – say it Spanish

3. Vivir (*bib-eer*)   to live

Yo _____/_ tu _____/el/ella _____/Nosotros _____,

vosotros _____,/ ellos/ellas _____,

4. Subir (*soo-beer*)   to go up / raise / increase

Yo _____/_ tu _____ /el/ella _____/,Nosotros _____

vosotros _____, / ellos/ellas _____,

5. Unir (*oo-neer*)   to unite, join

Yo _____,/ tu _____/ elel/la _____,/Nosotros _____

vosotros _____,/ ellos/ellas _____,

6. Decidir (*deth-ee-deer*)   to decide

Yo _____/ tu _____/ el/ella _____/,Nosotros _____,

vosotros _____/, ellos/ellas _____,

7. Recibir (*reth-ee-beer*)   to receive

Yo _____ / tu _____ / el/ella _____,/Nosotros _____

vosotros _____, /ellos/ellas _____,

If 5 out of 6 are correct,
class that one as correct.
If total less than 5, go back, and try again.....

```
    _____
       7
```

See it – say it Spanish

6.. Fill in the blanks with either the **English** or **Spanish** form as required.........

(eg: decidi   I decide   / vives   you live .. / they write: escriben)

I argue _____/ decidis_____/ suben _____

they write_____/ he live's_____ / vivimos _____

we quarrel _____ / I receive _____/ we live_____

escribimos_____ / subo _____ / uñimos _____

she decides _____ / suben _____/ he writes _____

recibo _____/ he argues _____ / reciben _____

escribo _____ / sube _____

8 - 10   average
11 - 14   above average
15 - 20   excellent

20

So far you have practiced conjugating the **ar**, **er**, and **ir** verbs in the present tense separately.......well !! now we will try a mixture of all of those with a few new verbs thrown in.......this will prove to you that once you know the endings, they can be used to conjugate any verb...

See it – say it Spanish

Simply fill in the blanks as before in either the **English** or **Spanish** form as required....

Good luck !!
Remember ---***Puedo hacerlo*** ------
₋I CAN DO IT !!

Here is a mixture of **25** that you have already learnt..........

*(eg: corro: **I run**   / anda: **you walk** / they read: **leen**)*

I owe _____ / temeis _____

you talk _____ / hablamos _____

andan _____ / viven _____

You walk _____ / subo _____

uñen _____/ _Servis _____

we write _____ / corremos _____

He sells _____ / escribes _____

you read _____ / rompen _____ __

See it – say it Spanish

decidimos _____ / I sing _____

debemos _____ / roban _____

you all decide _____ / temes _____

corro _____ / we eat _____

nadamos _____

_____

25

8 - 12   average
13 - 19   above average
19 - 25   excellent

New verbs

Cenar	- to dine; evening meal	(*th-en-aah*)
Esperar	- to wait	(*ess-pe-raah*)
Seperar	- to separate	(*sep-e-raah*)
Llevar	- to take or to wear	(*yev-aah*)
Llegar	- to arrive	(*ye-gaah*)
Pagar	- to pay for	(*pa-gaah*)
Desear	- to wish, want or desire	(*des-ay-aah*)
Beber	- to drink	(*beb-air*)
Aprender	- to learn	(*ap-rend-air*)
Creer	- to believe, think	(*cree-air*)
Ver	- to see, watch, look at	(*b-air*)
Abrir	- to open	(*abb-reer*)
Aburrir	- to bore, annoy, vex	(*abb-urr-eer*)
Permitir	- to allow, permit	(*per-mit-eer*)
Sufrir	- to suffer, tolerate	(*suff-reer*)

See it – say it Spanish

Well done !! now for the next **40**, and they are **all** from **verbs** that you have not learnt yet, don't be afraid.... simply apply the endings appropriate to that verb.....

oh ! forgot to add... to say the verb in the *negative* (**negativo** -neg-at-eebo)..just put 'no' before the conjugation....

Eg. **Corres** - *you run.*
No *corres* - *you don't run / don't run*
Hablamos - *we talk.*
No *hablamos* - *we don't talk / don't talk*

abro _____ / llevan _____

aprendo _____ / we wait _____

no pago _____ / I don't allow _____

No sufrimos _____ / they drink _____

llegamos _____ / seperas _____

deseo _____ / crees _____

they learn _____ / we see _____

permitimos _____ / llegas _____

See it – say it Spanish

no abrís _____ / bebo _____

veo _____ / Aprendemos _____

aburres _____ / desean _____

They think _____ / no pagas _____

I wear _____ / llevas _____

no crees _____ / we wish _____

cenamos _____ / you all learn _____

sufro _____ / No esperan _____

aburrimos _____ / they permit _____

We dine _____ / beben _____

you all take _____ / **No** deseamos _____

They don't pay _____ /Creemos _____

10- 20   average
21 - 30   above average
31 - 40   excellent

40

See it – say it Spanish

Well.how was that ?...... not so frightening as you thought. It was a lot to attempt in such a short space of time....but I have faith that *'puede hacerlo'* you can do it, and you should be proud of yourself for how you have progressed so far since the beginning of the book.

Bueno para saber' - *Good to know's'*
(*bwen-oh para sab-bare*)

When the Spanish meet they use one of 2 greetings:
'hola ¿que tal? (*kay-tal*) Or *'hola ¿como estas?* (*comb-o estas*), Both mean how are you, however when *'que tal'* is used the person does not expect much of an answer except *'bien gracias'* (*bee-enn grath-ee-ass*) or *'muy bien gracias'*. *(very well thank you)'* when *'como estas'* is used the person wants to know and expects to be told. When someone is passing another but not stopping, they will either say
'hasta luego'
(asta loo-ay-go) or
'adios' (*add-ee-oss*)

Lo sabias....

Que tal	how are you
Como estas	how are you
Bien	well
Muy bien	very well
Gracias	thank you
Hasta luego	until later
Adios	hello & / or goodbye

See it – say it Spanish

You need to be aware that there are some verbs, called *'irregular verbs*, that are a little harder to learn. These are verbs that for one reason or another do not follow the normal pattern that you have learnt so far. These will be covered in the 2nd book in this series....

see you there !!

........X-SEARCH......

Now for a bit of fun......I have combined the joys of a **'crossword puzzle'** with the frustration of a **'word search'**, to form **'cross-search'**.

Within the grid box are what seems, like row's and row's of random letter's, they are however very cleverly concealed English & Spanish words or verbs.

Your mission (*should you choose to accept it* !) soz !...just watched ' **Mission Impossible** ' lol, is to firstly look at the clue's to define the word or verb that you are searching for, secondly scan the grid for them, once found draw a circle around it and continue until all are found. Use a pencil, as this will allow you to erase and reuse at a later

See it – say it Spanish

date.....the more proficient you become with your Spanish, the quicker you will be able to complete the **'Cross-Search**

The clues and the answers are in English and / or Spanish
The answers can either be horizontal, vertical or diagonal

Here is a simple taster as an example: *(Regular verbs)*

C	O	R	R	E	R	Q
A	V	O	G	L	V	L
M	A	B	W	Q	S	I
B	C	A	N	T	A	R
I	A	R	O	G	I	L
A	B	R	I	R	O	U
R	V	I	V	E	I	S
W	E	T	A	L	K	B
Y	O	U	H	I	R	E
O	W	E	W	L	S	B
W	I	Q	S	U	O	O

To run   I drink
To change   alquilas
to rob/steal   Hablamos
To sing   You all live
Deber

See it – say it Spanish

This one is all regular verbs.........ENJOY !!

A	L	Q	U	I	L	A	R	T	J	C	R	E	E	R
P	G	A	I	L	R	W	B	B	K	F	A	O	E	E
R	A	W	R	U	P	U	U	S	X	V	N	V	W	S
E	D	S	F	P	C	E	N	A	R	W	X	R	C	P
N	O	E	E	T	Y	U	M	D	J	O	A	W	H	O
D	A	P	O	A	G	S	G	I	R	B	J	T	B	N
E	U	E	O	T	R	I	F	S	O	G	I	U	K	D
R	W	R	O	H	S	W	H	R	F	I	O	Z	Z	E
K	L	A	S	B	Y	O	Q	E	A	V	E	L	H	R
E	O	R	D	N	B	R	A	Z	E	Y	L	C	T	E
A	B	C	T	K	E	I	B	R	L	V	W	T	H	C
R	M	N	U	E	P	A	W	H	E	E	I	V	W	O
A	E	L	L	E	G	A	R	I	O	T	U	V	B	M
X	J	H	M	B	S	I	H	T	E	O	G	T	I	E
P	E	R	M	I	T	I	R	O	H	A	B	L	A	R

Clues

To hire / rent -
To answer/respond -
To learn -   To live -To take - To talk
To rob/steal - To believe -
To allow - To read - To see- To eat
To separate - To walk (for pleasure)

See it – say it Spanish

This one is conjugated regular verbs....enjoy !

H	A	B	L	A	M	O	S	D	W	Y	U	O	V	D
A	W	U	D	E	N	A	S	E	A	O	M	S	T	E
B	E	L	K	A	E	E	G	S	E	E	N	Y	H	S
L	O	P	E	T	Y	B	J	E	A	F	G	H	I	E
A	U	R	E		E	N	O	A	C	R	E	E	S	A
L	L	E	H	O	I	N	T	W	O	V	T	O	I	M
S	O	H	G	E	O	N	E	Y	M	O	N	A	D	O
O	H	R	E	S	P	O	N	D	E	I	S	O	S	S
M	E	O	S	T	I	O	C	H	N	T	S	G	N	I
I	H	E	C	O	M	E	M	O	S	O	E	S	E	N
T	A	G	R	E	E	D	T	I	M	V	V	I	S	E
I	B	H	I	O	P	E	R	M	I	T	E	N	O	A
P	U	O	B	S	A	N	D	V	O	I	S	R	G	O
E	O	S	E	F	R	O	B	S	E	A	O	M	T	H
R	R	I	S	S	F	C	E	A	S	N	A	B	O	R

Clues

We talk   -   you write   -
 they argue   - They eat
He talks   -   she believes   -
they permit - They rob/steal   -
we wish   -   he desires
You all answer   -   we repeat   -
 she lives - I swim   -   we eat

END OF LESSON DRILLS

FINAL PRACTICE.
We will now put it altogether for a final practice.......

1   verb drills...
remember...

.a.   drop the '**ar**', '**er**' or '**ir**' and add the appropriate endings
'**ar**'....... *o, as, a, amos, ais, an*
'**er**'....... *o, es, e, emos, eis, en*
'**ir**' .... *o, es, e, imos, ís, en*
b.   the stress/emphasis is on the last vowel in the full verb, and   on the last but one (penultimate) vowel of the conjugated verb...

eg, '**ar**'   esperar (to wait - **es-pair-rah**)
eg: **abrir (ab-r-eer)**.... to open
Yo __**ABRO**_____, tu __**ABRES**_____, el/ella **ABRE**__
Nosotros _**ABREMOS**, vosotros _**ABREIS**__, ellos/ellas __**ABREN**___,

'ar'   **Abandonar** (to abandon - ***a-ban-don-ah***)

yo _____, tu _____, el/ella _____,

Nosotros _____, vosotros _____, ellos/ellas _____,

'er'   **Aprender** (to learn - ***ap-rend-air***)

Yo _____, tu _____, el/ella _____,

Nosotros _____, vosotros _____, ellos/ellas _____,

See it – say it Spanish

'ir'   **escribir** (to write - ***es-crib-eer)***

Yo _____, tu _____, el/ella _____

Nosotros _____, vosotros _____, ellos/ellas _____

'ar'   **Hablar** (to talk - ***ab-lah)***

Yo _____, tu _____, el/ella _____,

Nosotros _____, vosotros _____, ellos/ellas _____,

'er'   **Deber** (to owe - ***de-bair)***

Yo _____, tu _____, el/ella _____,

Nosotros _____, vosotros _____, ellos/ellas _____

'ir'   **Insistir** (to insist – ***een-sist-eer)***

Yo _____, tu _____, el/la _____,

Nosotros _____, vosotros _____, ellos/ellas _____,

'er'   **Vender** (to sell – ***ben-d-air)***

Yo _____, tu _____, el/ella _____,

Nosotros _____, vosotros _____, ellos/ellas _____

See it – say it Spanish

'ar' **Reformar** (to reform / Improve – *ref-or-mah*)

Yo _____, tu _____, el/ella _____

Nosotros _____, vosotros _____, ellos/ellas _____,

'ir' **Vivir** (to live – *bib-eer*)

Yo _____, tu _____, el/ella _____,

Nosotros _____, vosotros _____, ellos/ellas _____

'er' **Creer** (to believe – *cree-air*)

Yo _____, tu _____, el/la _____

Nosotros _____ vosotros _____, ellos/ellas _____,

9 -10	excellelent
4 – 8	average
0 – 4	possibly a need to re-learn some aspects and try again

$$\frac{}{10}$$

2. mixed conjugations for translation.......

Here are a number of mixed conjugations....simply insert the translation in either the English and / or the Spanish form as required.....

44

See it – say it Spanish

Verb + form	Spanish	English
Eg: **Esperar** *(nosotros)*	ans **esperamos**	& **we wait / hope**
Aprender (ellos)	ans _____	& _____
Abandonar (tu)	ans _____	& _____
Reñir (nosotros)	ans _____	& _____
Permitir (vosotros)	ans _____	& _____
Beber (yo)	ans _____	& _____
Hablar (vosotros)	ans _____	& _____
Escribir (la)	ans _____	& _____
Llevar (ellas)	ans _____	& _____
Creer (el)	ans _____	& _____
Separar (tu)	ans _____	& _____
Desear (yo)	ans _____	& _____
Responder (nosotros)	ans _____	& _____
Repitir (yo)	ans _____	& _____
Decidir (nosotros)	ans _____	& _____
Llegar (el)	ans _____	& _____

15 excellent / 8 – 13 average
00 – 7 possibly a need to re-learn some aspects
of the book and try again

15

See it – say it Spanish

3. I know it's only book 1 and you have not had much time to assimilate all that you have learnt...but let's see how you are with the numbers,

Listed here are a random set of numbers..the idea is that you write out fully how you would say them...

eg: 14.   catorce
          74.   Setenta y cuatro
          268   dos cientos sesenta y ocho

Give them a try...

1. 13_____
2. 27_____
3. 82_____
4. 97_____
5. 25_____
6. 61_____
7. 43_____
8. 91_____

See it – say it Spanish

9. 58 _____

10. 100 _____

9 -10   excellelent
4 – 8   average
0 – 4   possibly a need to re-learn some
        Spects of the numbers and try again

```
┌─────────────┐
│             │
│             │
│    ____     │
│     10      │
└─────────────┘
```

Ok…. so you thought that was easy…. lets try some a little more complicated….

1. 164 _____
2. 106 _____
3. 258 _____
4. 358 _____
5. 296 _____
6. 837 _____
7. 592 _____
8. 756 _____
9. 586 _____
10. 703 _____

See it – say it Spanish

??? just try.....

11. 1,865 _____

12. 3,698 _____

13. 5,007 _____

14. 1060 _____

10 - 14   excellelent
5 - 9   average
0 – 4   possibly a need to re-learn some aspects of the numbers and try again

14

Buenos para saber (bwen-oss para sa-b-air) good to know

In Spanish, arithmatic (***aritmética a-rit-me-tee-ka***)
the following terms are used:
For ***multiplication:*** 'por' eg: *5 x 3 = 15* / cinco <u>por</u> tres son quince
For ***subtraction:*** 'menos' eg: *15 – 5 = 10* / quince <u>menos</u> cinco son diez
For ***addition:*** 'plus' or 'y' eg: *4 + 7 = 11* / cuatro <u>plus</u> siete son once / cuatro <u>y</u> siete son once
For ***division:*** 'divider por' eg: *9 ÷ 3 = 3* / nueve <u>divider por</u> tres son tres

Son (s-on) means 'they are' / if the answer is the number 1 then use 'es' *(it is)*

SUMMARY.

OK, during the course of this 1st book you have covered a number of things including:

1. The Spanish alphabet, how to pronounce the letters of the alphabet and the rules with respect to certain letters and letter combinations.
2. The Spanish numbering system and how to pronounce them.
3. How to conjugate *'ar'*, *'er'* and *'ir'* regular verbs in the present tense, where and how to apply the stress vowel for verbs and conjugations. This you have practiced both by the use of verb drills applicable to *'ar,' 'er',& 'ir'* verbs, and by the translation of conjugated verbs in English and Spanish.
4. you had a consolidated practice by using a mixture of *'ar', 'er', & 'ir'* verbs already learnt, along with verbs that you had not seen before.
5. You also had a little fun with the X-search puzzles.
6. You also learnt a few odd facts about the Spanish and their language with the *'buenos para saber'* boxes.

All in all you have covered quite a lot.....and you should give yourself a round of applause / pat on the back, ...a famous Chinese proverb say's...*'a journey of a thousand miles begins with the first step'* and this is just the
<u>first step in **your** journey</u>......so !

'Bon voyage' (oops !! ...thats French..sorry ! .lol)

Most important of all, is that, I really hope I have given you a taste to want to learn more, and enjoy the satisfaction of being able to speak to the Spanish people in their own language with confidence and.... be understood.

LOOK FORWARD.....

Fantastic !!!..well done you... Well, that is the 1st book completed...remember that you can (and should) return to this book as often as you feel necessary, if only to self test and reassure yourself. After 14 years I still return to the literature and notebooks that I used from the beginning. we learn a lot. But! Without constant or regular use it is so easy to forget..

.......See it – Say it ..... Spanish......

See it – say it Spanish

Lets see what's coming up as we look forward to the 2nd book in this series where you can continue to learn in a simple, easy to understand, and enjoyable way ..
In book 2 you will learn about...

1. ***irregular 'ar', 'er', 'ir'*** verbs in the present tense.
    i. Stem changing verbs
    ii. yo – go verbs
    iii. Sound changer's
2. **_Reflexive 'ar', 'er', & 'ir' verbs_**
3. **_Haber, '...ado' , '...ido', '...ando', & '...iendo'._**
4. **_Ser and estar_**
5. **Telling the time**
6. **Days, months and seasons of the year**
7. **Useful phrases for use in shops /bars /cafés**

Remember : **recordar** (*reck-cor-dah*)   to remember

'PUEDO HACERLO' !!!

See it – say it Spanish

COMMON REGULAR VERB LIST

Listed below is a common list of some of the much used regular verbs that you could use frequently………By applying the relative *ar*, *er*, *ir* endings it is possible for you to conjugate and use confidently all of these verbs….

Verb	meaning	how to say it
Agitar	to shake / stir	(*a-khit-ah*)
Ahorrar	to save	(*a-orr-rah*)
Añadir	to add	(**an-yad-eer**)
Aprender	to learn	(***ap-rend-air***)
Ayudar	to help / assist / aid	(**ay-you-dah**)
bañar	to bathe (take a bath)	(***ban-yah***)
Buscar	to search / seek / look for	(***bus-kah***)
Cansar	to be tired	(**can-sah**
cantar	to sing	(***can-tah***)
Cenar	to dine	(***then-ah***)
Comprar	to buy	(***kom-pr-ah***)
Contestar	to answer	(***kon-test-ah***)
Cortar	to cut	(***kor-tah***)

See it – say it Spanish

Verb	meaning	how to say it
Descansar	to rest / relax	(**dess-can-sah**)
Desear	to wish/want/desire	(**des-ay-yah**)
Disfrutar	to enjoy	(**diss-froot-ah**)
duchar	to shower	(**dooch-ah**)
Escribir	to write	(**ess-cree-beer**)
Esperar	to wait / hope	(**ess-pe-rah**)
Fumar	to smoke	(**foo-mah**)
Ganar	to win / earn	(**ga-nah**)
Gastar	to spend (money)	(**gas-tah**)
Hablar	to talk	(**ab-lah**)
Incluir	to include	(**een-cloo-eer**)
lavar	to wash	(**la-bah**)
Leer	to read	(**lee-air**)
limpiar	to clean	(**limp-ee-ah**)
Llamar	to call by voice / telephone	(**yam-ah**)
Llegar	to arrive	(**ye-gah**)
Llenar	to fill	(**yen-ah**)
Llevar	to take / wear	(**ye-bah**
Mirar	to watch	(**mee-rah**)
Nadar	to swim	(**na-dah**)
Pagar	to pay for	(**pa-gar**)
Pasar	to spend (time)	(**passah**)

See it – say it Spanish

Verb	meaning	how to say it
Preguntar	to ask a question	**(pre-gun tar)**
Quedar	to remain / stay	**(ked-dah)**
Quitar	to remove	**(kit-ah)**
Recibir	to receive	**(reth-ee-beer)**
Reparar	to repair	**(rep-a-rah)**
Responder	to respond / answer	**(ress-pond-air)**
Robar	to rob / steal	**(roe-bah)**
Sacar	to take out (something)	**(sac-kah)**
Terminar	to finish	**(term-in-ah)**
Tirar	to pull /throw	**(tee-rah)**
Tomar	to take (food/drink)	**(toe-mah)**
Trabajar	to work	**(trab-a-khah)**
Tratar	to treat	**(trat-ah)**
Vender	to sell	**(ben-dair)**
Visitor	to visit	**(bis-it-ah)**

ANSWERS

Ans for page 22, AR verb drills

1. Cantar
Yo, canto. / tu, cantas / el/la, canta / nosotros, cantamos / vosotros, cantais / ellos/ellas, cantan

2. andar
Yo, ando. / tu, andas / el/la, anda / nosotros, andamos / vosotros, andais / ellos/ellas, andan

3. bailar
Yo, bailo. / tu, bailas / elo/la, baila / nosotros, bailamos / vosotros, bailais / ellos/ellas, bailan

4. nadar
Yo, nado. / tu, nadas / el/la, nada / nosotros, nadamos / vosotros, nadais / ellos/ellas, nadan

5. tratar
Yo, trato. / tu, tratas / el/la, trata / nosotros, tratamos / vosotros, tratais / ellos/ellas, tratan

6. pasear
Yo, paseo. / tu, paseas / el/la, pasea / nosotros, paseamos / vosotros, paseais / ellos/ellas, pasean

7. robar
Yo, robo. / tu, robas / el/la, roba / nosotros, robamos / vosotros, robais / ellos/ellas, roban

Ans for page 24, AR conjugations

I sing *canto* / andas *you walk* / tratan *they treat* / they rob *roban*

He *trata* / pasean *they walk* / we sing *cantamos* / I walk *paseo*

Bailais *you all dance* / nada *he/she/it swims* / we dance *bailamos* / trato *I treat*

Andan *they walk_* / paseais *you all walk* / she robs *roba* / we swim *nadamos*

Nadas *you swim* / They walk *andan* / robo *I rob* / tratamos *we treat*

Ans for page 26, ER verb drills

1.vender
Yo, vendo. / tu, vendes / el/la, vende / nosotros, vendemos / vosotros, vendeis / ellos/ellas, venden

2.leer
Yo, leo. / tu lees / el/la, lee / nosotros, leemos / vosotros, leeis / ellos/ellas, leen

3.correr
Yo, corro / tu, corres / el/la, corre / nosotros, corremos / vosotros, correis / ellos/ellas, corren

4.deber
Yo, debo. / tu, debes / el/la, debe / nosotros, debemos / vosotros, debeis / ellos/ellas, deben

5.romper
Yo, rompo / tu, rompes / el/la, rompe / nosotros, rompemos / vosotros, rompeis / ellos/ellas, rompen

6.responder
Yo, respondo. / tu, respondes / el/la, responde / nosotros, respondemos / vosotros, respondeis
 ellos/ellas, responden

7.temer
Yo, temo. / tu, temes / el/la, teme / nosotros, tememos / vosotros,temeis / ellos/ellas, temen

Ans for page 28,   ER conjugations

I sell- *vendo* / corres -*you run* / leen -*they read* / they broke- *rompen*
He breaks -*rompe* / respondeis -*you all answer* / we run- *corremos* /
I read -*leo* / rompemos- *we broke* / debe- *he/she/It owe* /
we reply- *respondemos* / vendemos- *we sell*
tememos- *we are afraid* / corren- *they run* / she is afraid- *teme* /
we owe *debemos* / lees *you read*   / They sell *venden* /
responde -*he/she/it reply* / leemos- *we read*

ans for page, 30   IR verb drills

1.reñir
Yo, reño. / tu, reñes / el/la, reñe / nosotros, reñimos / vosotros, reñis / ellos/ellas, reñen
2.escribir
Yo, escribo. / tu, escrides / el/la, escribe / nosotros, escribimos / vosotros, escribis / ellos/ellas escriben
3.vivir
Yo, vivo. / tu, vives/ el/la, vive / nosotros, vivimos / vosotros, vivis / ellos/ellas, viven
4.subir
Yo, subo. / tu, subes / el/la, sube / nosotros, subimos / vosotros, subis / ellos/ellas, suben
5.ynie
Yo, uno. / tu, unes / el/la, une / nosotros, unimos / vosotros, unis / ellos/ellas, unen
6.decidir
Yo, decido / tu, decides / el/la, decide / nosotros, decidimos / vosotros, decidís / ellos/ellas, deciden
7.recibirr
Yo, recibo. / tu, recibes / el/la, recibe / nosotros, decidimos / vosotros, decidís / ellos/ellas, deciden

See it – say it Spanish

Ans for page 32, IR conjugations

I argue *reño* / decidis *we decide* / suben *they raise* / they write *escriben*

he lives *vive* / vivimos *we live* / we quarrel *reñimoss* / I receive *recibo*

escribimos *we write* / subo *I go up* / we live *vivimos* / unimos *we unite, join*

she decides *decide* / suben *they go up* / he writes *escribe* / recibo *I receive*

he argues *rene* / reciben *they receive* / escribo *I write* / sube *he raises*

Ans for page 33, mixed conjugations

I owe, *debo* / temeis, *you all are afraid* / you talk, *hablas* /

hablamos, *we talk* / Andan, *they walk* / viven, *they live* /

You walk, *andas* / subo *I go up, raise* / Uñen, *they unite, join* /

Servís, *you all serve* / we write, *escribimos* / corremos, *we run*

He sells, *vendes* / escribes, *you write* / you read, *lees* /

rompen, *they break, tear* / Decidimos, *we decide* / I sing, *canto* /

debemos, *we owe* / roban, *they rob, steal* / you all decide, *decidís* /

temes, *you are afraid* / corro, *I run* / we eat, *comemos* /

See it – say it Spanish

nadamos, *we swim*

ans for page 35, mixed conjugations

Abro, *I open* / llevan, *they take-wear* / aprendo, *I learn* /

we wait, *esperamos* / no pago, *I don't pay* / I don't allow, *no permito* /

No sufrimos, *we don't suffer* / they drink, *beben* / llegamos, *we arrive* /

eperas, *you separate* / deseo, *I wish, desire, want*

crees, *you believe, think* / they learn, *aprendemos* / we see, *vimos*

permitimos, *we permit, allow* / llegas, *you arrive* / no abris, *you don't open*

bebo, *I drink* / veo, *I see* / Aprendemos, *we learn* / aburres, *you bore, annoy*

desean, *they, desire, wish* / They think, *creen* / no pagas, *you don't pay*

I wear, *llevo* / Llevas, *you take, wear* / no crees, *you don't believe, think*

we wish, *deseamos* / Cenamos, *we dine* / you all learn, *aprendeis*

sufro, *I suffer,* / No esperan, *they don't wait* / aburrimos, *we bore, annoy,*

they permit, *permiten* / We dine, *cenamos* / beben, *they drink*

you all take, *llevais* / No deseamos, *we don't desire, wish, want*

They don't pay, *no pagan* / Creemos, *we believe, think*

See it – say it Spanish

ans for X-SEARCH........ page 39

X-SEARCH........

C	O	R	R	E	R	Q
A	V	O	G	L	V	L
M	A	B	W	Q	S	I
B	C	A	N	T	A	R
I	A	R	O	G	I	L
A	B	R	I	R	O	U
R	V	I	V	E	I	S
W	E	T	A	L	K	B
Y	O	U	H	I	R	E
O	W	E	W	L	S	B
W	I	Q	S	U	O	O

To run / alquilas / To sing / to open
To change / to rob/steal / You all live
I drink / Hablamos / deber

See it – say it Spanish

ans for X-SEARCH........ page 40

2. This one is all full verbs.......

A	L	Q	U	I	L	A	R	T	J	C	R	E	E	R
P	G	A	I	L	R	W	B	B	K	F	A	O	E	E
R	A	W	R	U	P	U	U	S	X	V	N	V	W	S
E	D	S	F	P	C	E	N	A	R	W	X	R	C	P
N	O	E	E	T	Y	U	M	D	J	O	A	W	H	O
D	A	P	O	A	G	S	G	I	R	B	J	T	B	N
E	U	E	O	T	R	I	F	S	O	G	I	U	K	D
R	W	R	O	H	S	W	H	R	F	I	O	Z	Z	E
K	L	A	S	B	Y	O	Q	E	A	V	E	L	H	R
E	O	R	D	N	B	R	A	Z	E	Y	L	C	T	E
A	B	C	T	K	E	I	B	R	L	V	W	T	H	C
R	M	N	U	E	P	A	W	H	E	E	I	V	W	O
A	E	L	L	E	V	A	R	I	O	T	U	V	B	M
X	J	H	M	B	S	I	H	T	E	O	G	T	I	E
P	E	R	M	I	T	I	R	O	H	A	B	L	A	R

To hire / rent - To answer/respond - To allow
To believe - To read - to separate - To learn
To rob/steal - To live - To see - To talk
To eat - To walk (for pleasure) - to take
To dine

See it – say it Spanish

ans for X-SEARCH........ page 41

X-SEARCH........

3. This one is conjugated *ar*, *er* & *ir* verbs only.....

H	A	B	L	A	M	O	S	D					
A								E					E
B							S						S
L							E						E
A		R	E	Ñ	E	N		A	C	R	E	E	S	A
								O					M
S								M		N	A	D	O
O		R	E	S	P	O	N	D	E	I	S		S
M			S					N					
I			C	O	M	E	M	O	S		E		
T			R						M	V			
I			I		P	E	R	M	I	T	E	N		
P			B				V						
E			E										
R			S						N	A	B	O	R

We talk - you write - they argue - He talks
she believes - they permit - They rob/steal
we wish - he desires - You all answer - we repeat
she lives - They eat

62

See it – say it Spanish

Ans for page 42 mixed verb drills

Answers for End of lesson drills....
Verb drills..

1.Abandonar
Yo *abandano*, / tu , *abandonas,* / lo/la, *abandona,* / Nosotros , *abandonamos,* / vosotros, *abandonais*
ellos/ellas, *abandonan,*

2. Aprender
Yo *aprendo* / tu, *aprendes,* / el/la, *aprende,* / Nosotros, *aprendemos,* / vosotros, *aprendeis,* ellos/ellas, *aprenden*

3.escribir
Yo *escribo,* / tu *escribes,* / el/la , *escribe,* / nosotros ,*escribimos* / vosotros *escribís,* ellos/ellas *escriben*

4. Hablar
Yo *hablo,* / tu , *hablas* / el/la *habla* / Nosotros , *Hablamos,* / vosotros , *hablais,* ellos/ellas , *hablan*

5.Deber
Yo *debo,* / tu ,*debes,* / el/la *debe,* / Nosotros, *debemos,* / vosotros ,*debeis,* , ellos/ellas *deben*

6.Insistir
'Yo *insisto,* / tu , *insistes* / el/la *insiste,* / Nosotros *insistimos,* / vosotros , *insistís,* ellos/ellas, *insisten*

See it – say it Spanish

.7.Vender
Yo *vendo,* / tu, *vendes,* / el/la, *vende,* / Nosotros , *vendemos,* / vosotros , *vendeis* ellos/ellas, *venden*

8.Reformar
'Yo *reformo* / tu, *reformas,* / el/la, *reforma* / Nosotros , *reformamos* / vosotros , *reformais*
ellos/ellas *reforman*

9.Vivir
Yo *vivo* / tu , *vives,* / el/la, *vive,* / Nosotros , *vivimos,* / vosotros , *vivís* ellos/ellas , *viven*

10.Creer
Yo *creo,* / tu, *crees,* / el/la, *cree,* / nosotros , *creemos* / vosotros , *creeis* ellos/ellas, *creen*

ans for page 45,

Verb + form	Spanish	English
Aprender (ellos)	ans *aprenden*	& *they learn (male or mixed)*
Abandonar (tu)	ans: *abandonas*	& *we abandon*
Reñir (nosotros)	ans: *reñimos*	& *we argue / quarrel*
Permitir (vosotros)	ans: *permiteis*	& *you all permit*
Beber (yo)	ans: *bebo*	& *I drink*

See it – say it Spanish

Verb + form	Spanish	English
Hablar (vosotros)	ans: **hablais**	& *you all talk*
Escribir (la)	ans: **escribe**	& *she writes*
Llevar (ellas)	ans: **llevan**	& *they take (female)*
Creer (el)	ans: **cree**	& *he believes*
Separar (tu)	ans: **separas**	& *you separate*
Desear (yo)	ans: **deseo**	& *I wish / deire*
Responder (nosotros)	ans: **respondemos**	& *we respond / answer*
Repitir (yo)	ans: **repito**	& *I repeat*
Decidir (nosotros)	ans: **decidimos**	& *we decide*
Llegar (el)	ans: **llega**	& *he arrives*

See it – say it Spanish

Ans for Page 46, numbers

Listed here are a random set of numbers..the idea is that you write out fully how you would say them…

Give them a try…

1.	13	trece	(treth-ay)
2.	27	veintisiete	(bent-ee ee say-ay-tay)
3.	82	ochenta y dos	(otch-enta ee d-os)
4.	97	noventa y siete	(no-benta ee say-ay-tay)
5.	25	veinticinco	(bent-ee ee th-een-co)
6.	61	sesenta y uno	(sess-enta ee oo-no)
7.	43	cuarenta y tres	(kwar-enta ee tress)
8.	91	noventa y uno	(no-benta e oo-no)
9.	58	cincuenta y ocho	(theen-kwenta ee ot-cho)
10	100	cien	(th-ee-en)

See it – say it Spanish

Ans for Page 47

Ok.... so you thought that was easy.... lets try some a little more complicated....

1. 164   ciento sesenta y cuatro   *(th-ee-ento sess-enta ee kwat-roe)*

2. 106   ciento seis   *(th-ee-ento says)*

3. 258   doscientos cinquenta y ocho
        (doss-th-ee-entos theen-kwenta ee ot-cho)

4. 358   tres-thee-entos cincuenta y ocho
        (tres-th-ee-entos theen-kwenta ee ot-cho)

5. 296   doscientos noventa y seis
        (doss-th-ee-entos no-benta ee says)

6. 837   ochocientos trienta y siete
        (ot-cho-th-ee-entos tree-enta ee say-ay-tay)

7. 592   *quinientos noventa y dos* *(kin-ee-entos no-benta ee doss)*

8. 756   sietecientos cincuenta y sies
        (say-ay-tay-th-ee-entos then-kwenta-ee sayss)

9. 586   quinientos ochenta *y sies* *(kin-ee-entos otch-enta ee says)*

10. 703   sietecientos tres   *(say-ay-tay-th-ee-entos tress)*

See it – say it Spanish

??? just try.....

11.. *1,865*   mil ochocientos sesenta y cinco
    (meel ot-cho-th-ee-entos sess-enta ee then-co)

12. *3,698*   tres mil siescientos noventa y ocho
    (tress-meel sayss-th-ee-entos no-benta ee ot-cho)

13. *5,007*   cinco meel siete   *(then-co-m-eel say-ay-tay)*

14. 1060   mil sesenta   *(meel sess-enta)*

ABOUT THE AUTHOR:

John James (JJ) is a child of the 50's. The days when Education centred around the 3 'R's, **R**eading, w**R**iting and a**R**ithmatic. Everything learned had a practical day to day usefulness. There were no fancy lessons, especially languages. He left school, just barely 15 years old – directly into the workforce. Trying his hand at many things for a number of years, and becoming a bit of a *'jack of all trades – master of none'*, until in the mid 1970's, with a wife and a couple of kids, he decided To enlist into the Army, reaching the rank of 'Warrant Officer (WOII) and finally re-entering civvy street 5 years into the new millennium. He and his wife had a yearning to move to and live in Spain, so he attended at night school for basic Spanish...and found that it wasn't as scary as he thought. The move to Spain happened approx 15 months later. He has attended Spanish language classes since he arrived...always thinking that *'there has to be an easier way to do this'*....hence his foray into writing with this

'See it - Say it' **Basic Spanish** series, and an accompanying series **'Talk to me'** **conversation Spanish**, learn how the Spanish speak...but with a twist...

John has been married for 46 years with 5 kids and 13 grandkids and still lives in Spain.

See it – say it Spanish

See it – say it Spanish

Made in the USA
Middletown, DE
27 October 2025